CRIME
AND
CAPITAL
PUNISHMENT

ROBERT H. LOEB, JR.

IN
CONSULTATION
WITH

PROFESSOR
GEORGE F. COLE

CRIME
AND CAPITAL
PUNISHMENT

REVISED EDITION | AN IMPACT BOOK | 1986
FRANKLIN WATTS
NEW YORK | LONDON | SYDNEY | TORONTO

Photographs courtesy of UPI/Bettmann Newsphotos: pp. 11, 12, 58, 62, 67, 78; The New York Public Library Picture Collection: pp. 19, 20, 25, 26, 31, 39; AP/Wide World: pp. 42, 68, 71; Richmond Newspapers, Inc./Staff Photo: p. 45; Don Sturkey © 1985 The Charlotte Observer/The Charlotte News: p. 54; Southern Illinoisan Staff Photo: p. 57; The Charlotte Observer, Staff Photos by Davie Hinshaw: pp. 81, 82.

Library of Congress Cataloging-in-Publication Data

Loeb, Robert H.
Crime and capital punishment.

(An impact book)
Bibliography: p.
Includes index.
Summary: Presents an overview of the history of capital punishment theories on the causes of crime and the deterrent effects of punitive actions, and the moral and legal principles involved.
1. Capital punishment—History—Juvenile literature. 2. Crime and criminals—History—Juvenile literature. 3. Capital punishment—United States—Juvenile literature. [I. Capital punishment. 2. crime and criminals] I. Cole, George F., 1935-   . II. Title.
HV8694.L63   1987   364.6'6'09   86-13356
ISBN 0-531-10209-2

CONTENTS

CRIME
AND
CAPITAL
PUNISHMENT

1
CAPITAL PUNISHMENT— YES OR NO?

Capital punishment has been an emotionally charged issue in the United States for over two hundred years. This is understandable, since the deliberate taking of a human being's life, though sanctioned by law, is a drastic and irrevocable punishment. Opponents to the death penalty started making objections in the latter part of the eighteenth century. Not to abolish it for all crimes, but to reduce the number of crimes considered "capital offenses" (crimes which are punishable by death). The number of crimes labeled capital offenses in earlier times was astonishingly large.

The abolitionists (those opposing the death penalty) became increasingly dominant, and consequently their influence brought about some changes for the better. This resulted in a decrease in the number of crimes considered capital offenses. Eventually the number of executions in the United States dwindled to such an extent that by 1967, gassings, hangings, electrocutions, or death by firing squads had ceased completely. This suspension of legally sanctioned killings was the result of the efforts of the abolitionists' legal forces who appealed the legality of specific sentences in the state and federal courts. But in January 1977 the truce was shattered with a bang when Gary Mark Gilmore, a self-confessed murderer, was executed by a firing squad in Utah. This followed what can only be characterized as an obscene series of events. Gilmore insisted he be executed. However, the American Civil Liberties Union fought to save his life. He told them to "butt out." The man who wanted to be the first person executed in ten years became a hot news item. He was paid for interviews. Presses spewed out articles and books that had little or nothing to do with the legal or moral issues involved, but dwelt instead on the sensational and lurid aspects of the case.

Gilmore's execution undoubtedly had a terrifying impact on the several hundred people, in various states, who had been living in a state of suspension while awaiting adjudication (final determination) of their appeals from execution. But it did not start a rash of executions. It is likely that the circuslike atmosphere surrounding Gilmore's execution temporarily deterred further executions. In fact, Massachusetts, Kansas, New Mexico, and Hawaii rejected attempts to reinstitute capital punishment. Four months after Gilmore's execution only twenty-seven states allowed the death penalty.

However, this comparative truce did not last long. John Spenkelink, executed on May 25, 1979, was the first person to be executed in the United States against his will since 1967. There were three more executions following Spenkelink's. They were all consensual like Gilmore's. Jesse Walter Bishop, executed in Nevada on October 22, 1979, said: "Commute me or electrocute me. Don't drag it out." Another con-

A group of journalists is shown the
chair in which Gary Mark Gilmore was
executed by a firing squad in 1977.

For prisoners on death row, the Supreme Court's
rulings on the legality of death-penalty laws
are literally a matter of life and death.

demned man, executed in 1981 in Indiana, waived appeals and said he was sorry it happened. Two Supreme Court justices who voted against Bishop's execution called it "state administered suicide." But they were obviously in the minority. We shall examine this aspect when we go into the legal pros and cons of the death penalty in a subsequent section.

Where does the American public stand on the issue of the death penalty? In 1985 a Gallup poll showed that 72 percent were for it. In March 1981 a Gallup poll showed that 66 percent favored the death penalty for murder. However, we must question how well informed the American public is. Evidence that almost one-third are functionally illiterate and that most people depend in great part on television news handouts, might lead to some doubt about "majority" judgment. Assuredly, the fact that the majority of citizens favor capital punishment does not necessarily mean that it's the proper punishment for murder.

Nevertheless, executions are on the rise. Alpha Otis Stephens's execution in Georgia on December 12, 1984, was the twenty-second execution in twelve months in the United States, and during a one-year period, from December 1983 to December 1984, more than twice as many Americans were executed than in the previous twenty years. And the rate of executions is expected to grow. In 1985 there were 1,450 prisoners on death row in the thirty-eight states that permit capital punishment. Henry Schwarzschild, director of the capital punishment project for the American Civil Liberties Union, estimated that there would be fifty to sixty executions in 1985, saying, "The tumbrels [a reference to carts used during the French Revolution to transport condemned prisoners] are rolling."

Here is a state-by-state breakdown of executions from 1977 to March of 1985:

Alabama	1
Florida	12
Georgia	6
Indiana	1
Louisiana	7
Mississippi	1
Nevada	1
North Carolina	2
South Carolina	1
Texas	6
Utah	1
Virginia	2

The United States Supreme Court's decisions regarding the legality of capital punishment have been as sharp and clear-cut as if the wrong end of a knife had been used to cut a steak. In 1972, in the *Furman* v. *Georgia* decision, five members of the Court disallowed the imposition of the death penalty and four dissented. This decision centered on what constitutes "cruel and unusual punishment" within the meaning of the Eighth Amendment to the Constitution,* as applied to the states by the Fourteenth Amendment. That decision, in favor of the defendant, continued the abolitionists' ball rolling. But only temporarily, because subsequent decisions by the Court have created a great deal of legal confusion. It started with a 1976 Supreme Court decision that, in essence, permitted capital punishment under very loosely defined circumstances. It would seem that at present the Supreme Court is saying that capital punishment is constitu-

* "Amendment VIII: Excessive bail shall not be required, nor excessive fines imposed, nor cruel and unusual punishments inflicted."

tional. This gives the states the right to keep it, or reinstate it, and to apply it.

The purpose of this book is to give you background material so that you will be informed regarding the pros and cons involved in this issue. Forming an opinion about capital punishment involves three basic aspects of the issue: the moral factors (Is it just?), the legal factors (Is it administered according to the rules?), and the practical factors (Does it prevent crime?).

To begin the study, we shall look at the origins of capital punishment in early history, follow its manifestations in England prior to the eighteenth century, and then study its use in our country in colonial times. But learning about the origins of capital punishment is just the beginning. We must become acquainted with what criminologists and psychiatrists believe are the causes of violent social behavior. We must also become aware of the merits and demerits of our legal system. How just, impartial, and error-proof is it—particularly where it concerns those accused of capital offenses? With this background information you should be in a sound position to arrive at your own conclusion regarding the rightness or wrongness of the ultimate in punishment: the legal killing of a human being.

2

IN ANCIENT TIMES AND IN MERRY ENGLAND

The history of people's inhumanity to other people, in the name of crime prevention, retribution, and war, makes a mockery of our label—Homo "sapiens," or "thinking." There is no other living creature on earth that has shown such deliberate cruelty to its own or to other species.

During the past century we have made comparative progress in attitudes and practices toward those accused of crimes, and in our methods of crime prevention. But those who oppose capital punishment believe that, until the death penalty is abolished, we are guilty of archaic barbarism. Those opting for capital punishment feel that we have reduced the number of capital offenses to a bare minimum, transformed our methods of execution into painless surgery, and that to abolish such punishment would increase crime. What, if anything, is to be learned from the past?

CAPITAL OFFENSES
AND PUNISHMENT
IN ANCIENT TIMES

Egyptian records for 1750 B.C. describe trials of state criminals who were condemned to death. Mosaic law of around the seventh century B.C. contains precise references to capital offenses and prescribed methods of execution. For example, Deuteronomy 22:18–19 states, "If a man have a stubborn and rebellious son, which will not obey the voice of his father, or the voice of his mother . . . ," then the parent could bring the son before the city elders to describe his misdoings, and the elders "shall stone him with stones, that he die."

Deuteronomy 22:20–22 also says that if a husband, on his wedding night, discovers that his bride is not a virgin, then the elders could stone her to death.

About 450 B.C., under Roman law, vestal virgins (they were the guardians of certain temples) who violated their vows of chastity were sentenced to being burned alive. Under Roman law of the Twelve Tables, of the same era, the following crimes were considered capital offenses: publishing libels and insulting songs, stealing crops, arson, theft by a slave, perjury, willful murder of a freeman, and disturbing the peace in the city at night.

In the first century A.D. the Romans used crucifixion, drowning, beating to death, and burning alive

In biblical times, stoning was the punishment decreed for blasphemers and other miscreants.

as methods of execution, as had the Assyrians, Persians, Egyptians, Carthaginians, and Greeks earlier. No one people had a monopoly on barbarity.

Shameful to relate, the death penalty was used even more frequently after the advent of Christianity, despite its emphasis on mercy. The pre-Christian Barbaric Codes listed fewer capital crimes and milder punishments than western Europe's codes of the twelfth and thirteenth centuries. The most awful tortures and forms of execution were invented under religious auspices: rack and wheel, the iron maiden, and burning at the stake. Religious deviation was the most heinous crime and people (mostly women) accused of being witches were among those charged with that.

When the state eventually took over power from the church, it, too, used capital punishment to enforce authority and added some innovations of its own. For example, as late as 1812, in Merry England, when seven men were convicted of high treason, they were sentenced as follows: "That you and each of you, be taken to the place from whence you came, and from thence be drawn on a hurdle to the place of execution, where you shall be hanged by the neck not till you are dead, but that you be severally taken down, while yet alive, and your bowels be taken out and burned before your faces—that your heads be then cut off, and your bodies cut into four quarters, to be at the King's disposal. And God have mercy on your souls."

*In the middle ages, punishments
included drawing and quartering,
decapitation, and a wide variety
of other tortures.*

IN EARLY ENGLAND

In Anglo-Saxon times, under Saxon and Danish kings, the gallows was the most common form of execution. But beheading, burning, drowning, and stoning were also practiced. However, with the advent of William the Conqueror from France in the eleventh century, there came a surprising pause in use of the death penalty. William ordered that no person should be put to death for any offense. Criminals could be mutilated but not killed. This edict was not the result of humanitarian thinking but of practicality: fighting men were needed for his armies, whether criminals or not.

It wasn't long before the death penalty was reinstated—and with a vengeance. Practically every crime on the books became a capital offense. The list ranged from high and petty treason to all felonies (defined as "grave crimes"—an inadvertent, macabre pun): murder, manslaughter, arson, highway robbery, burglary, and larceny (stealing). The only exceptions were mayhem (deliberate maiming of another, depriving that person of fighting ability) and petty larceny (theft of property worth less than one shilling). The value of human life during the Middle Ages seems to have been worth little more than one shilling (about $1). In 1279, 280 Jews were hanged for "clipping coin" (debasing its value by shaving small amounts of metal from the coin). During the reign of England's King Edward I, in the same century, the mayor of Exeter and the porter of the town's south gate were executed because the gate had not been properly shut in time to prevent the escape of a criminal. Thus mass legalized killing for practically any transgression became the order of the day. This state of affairs remained in effect for centuries. Does this mean that crime must have been at a minimum? It wasn't.

What was the attitude of the church toward this indiscriminate killing? The only stand it took was to institute "benefit of clergy," which was a measure to protect clergymen. Originally this meant that no member of the clergy could be tried in a secular court, but its application was extended to anyone who was able to read and thus secure immunity from execution. Proof of literacy consisted of being able to read the Fifty-first Psalm, which became known as the "neck verse"—an appropriate title as hanging was the most common method of execution. Since most of the population was completely illiterate, not by accident but by the ruling powers' design, clerical immunity protected both the semiliterate clergy and aristocracy.

By the sixteenth century the state had usurped the church's power and applied capital punishment in a more "democratic" manner. In addition to the state's ordinary list of capital crimes, women (and on rare occasions, men) accused and found guilty of witchcraft were not hanged but burned alive. This horror was not exclusively England's but was practiced on the Continent as well. A German writer stated in 1845, "From the fifteenth to the beginning of the eighteenth century thousands of wretched witches were burned, and all on their own confession usually obtained by torture." W. F. Poole, a nineteenth-century American historian, in his book *Salem Witchcraft,* wrote that the death toll in Europe for witchcraft during the sixteenth and seventeenth centuries came to two hundred thousand.

Women were "honored" with additional forms of specialized punishment: ducking and drowning. These were not imposed for witchcraft, but for other "crimes." For example, in 1623, in Edinburgh, eleven Gypsy women were condemned to be drowned. On May 11, 1685, one Margaret M'Lachlan, aged sixty-three, and Margaret Wilson, eighteen, were drowned for denying that James II of England was entitled to rule the church.

Drawing and quartering, which we described earlier, was rather popular during the reign of Good Queen Bess (Elizabeth I). A number of recusant priests (Roman Catholic clergymen who refused to attend Anglican services) were executed in this brutal manner. On occasion the queen gave strict orders that victims should be conscious when the disembowelment began.

Sir Edward Coke (1552–1634), a chief justice of England, referred to by the *Encyclopaedia Brittanica* as "the greatest common lawyer of all times," justified drawing and quartering. He based this on a collection of biblical texts. Consequently, it became referred to as "godly butchery."

Sir William Blackstone (1723–80), considered in both England and America to be one of the greatest jurists of all times, saw nothing wrong with this form of punishment. He stated that there were few instances of people being disemboweled prior to being unconscious. However, some records belie this "justification."

By the time of George III, who reigned from 1760 to 1820, there were some 222 capital crimes listed on the statute books. Included were: stealing as little as 40 shillings ($40 in today's values), stealing from a shop the value of 5 shillings ($5), counterfeiting stamps used in the sale of perfumery and hair powder, and even cutting down a tree on someone else's property. In the late seventeenth and early eighteenth centuries, it was not uncommon for children under ten to be hanged. In one instance 10 ten-year-old boys were strung up as a warning to others. As late as 1808 a boy of eleven and a girl of seven were hanged for a felony.

Women accused of being witches were
often burned alive, as seen in this
sixteenth-century German illustration.

Criminals and heretics were often executed
in a public spectacle, as this sixteenth-century
English drawing shows.

Executions were usually public spectacles until the mid-nineteenth century. It was believed that public executions would by example deter crime. However, history shows that such publicity actually seems to have defeated its purpose. In the early nineteenth century, public hangings were occasions for sadistic celebrations where thieves and pickpockets joined the other onlookers in merriment. By the latter part of that century, it was finally recognized that such publicity served no deterrent purpose.

Progress! In England, by the beginning of the nineteenth century, the number of capital offenses was reduced to 200, and by 1823 this number was cut in half. This was not, however, because the crime rate had been effectively reduced through such generous use of the death penalty, but for quite a different reason. It began to dawn on the ruling powers that such frequent use of the death sentence appeared to be an act of futility and perhaps even of inhumanity in some cases.

3
FROM COLONIAL
TIMES TO 1986

The early American colonists did not quite duplicate the extreme anticrime methods of their mother country, England. Their number of capital offenses was fewer and their methods of execution were somewhat less sadistic. The earliest records from the Massachusetts Bay Colony, 1636, "The Capital Lawes of New-England," listed these "crimes" as worthy of the death sentence: idolatry, witchcraft, blasphemy, murder (excluding self-defense), assault in sudden anger, sodomy, buggery, adultery, statutory rape (death sentence optional), man-stealing, perjury in a capital trial, and rebellion.

The Bay Colony justified this list of capital offenses by citing the Old Testament's Mosaic law. It is sad to note that they disregarded the New Testament's principles, with particular reference to Christ's Sermon on the Mount (Matthew, chapter 5). Such neglect continues by many professing Christianity. All of which seems to make frighteningly valid the statement by the nineteenth-century philosopher Friedrich Nietzsche—that the last Christian died on the cross.

However, on a positive note, the Quaker colonists in South Jersey and Pennsylvania had far more humane attitudes. The Royal Charter (1646) listed no crime as worthy of the death penalty and there was no execution there for almost thirty years. Pennsylvania only imposed the death penalty for treason and murder. But by the eighteenth century, under direct orders from the Crown, all the colonies adopted harsh penal codes. By the time of the American Revolution, the majority of the colonies shared many similar capital statutes.

Dr. Benjamin Rush, a signer of the Declaration of Independence, was greatly influenced by a book *On Crime and Punishment,* by an Italian jurist, Cesare di Beccaria. Rush gave a lecture in Benjamin Franklin's home in which he recommended the construction of a penitentiary where criminals could be kept away from society and helped to overcome their antisocial habits. Dr. Rush is credited with being the founder of the movement to abolish capital punishment in the United States. In 1794, through the efforts of Benjamin Franklin and Attorney General William Bradford, the death penalty in Pennsylvania was repealed for all crimes except for murder in the "first degree (premeditated and planned)."

A distinguished American lawyer, Edward Livingston (1764–1836), also worked for the abolition of the death penalty, and by 1830 the movement gathered imposing momentum. Petitions were filed in many state legislatures and "anti-gallows" societies were formed on the eastern seaboard. In 1846 the territory of Michigan voted to abolish capital punishment for everything except treason and thus became the first jurisdiction in the English-speaking world to do so.

In the nineteenth-century American West, hanging was the most common method of execution.

The Civil War cooled off the abolitionist movement, as wars tend to encourage attitudes of violence. Prior to it, Tennessee, in 1838, made the death penalty optional for all capital offenses. In 1841 Alabama followed suit, as did Louisiana in 1846. Between the end of the Civil War and the dawn of the twentieth century, some twenty jurisdictions switched from mandatory to discretionary capital punishment. And from the beginning of the twentieth century until World War I, the movement gathered more strength. Between 1907 and 1917 nine states abolished the death penalty. But once again war, World War I, reversed this trend for a long time—forty years.

At the same time that abolition was slowly gaining acceptance, even before the beginning of the twentieth century, efforts were also being made to make executions "painless and swift" (although these are comparative descriptions as you will subsequently see). In the 1890s New York's electric chair became a nationally popular "best killer." In 1921 Nevada introduced lethal gas. It was to be administered "without warning" in the convicted person's cell. This does seem like a comparatively kindly idea, except that, if it had been tried, neighboring prisoners might have also faced eternity. The method for applying lethal gas was modified and more and more states adopted asphyxiation as a "gentle" form of killing. Nevada and Utah added shooting as another method.

By the middle of the twentieth century the death penalty was limited to first-degree murder and made *discretionary* in all U.S. jurisdictions.

As the chart on page 34 shows, abolition of the death penalty wasn't a winning cause, except in a few states. Among these were those with predominantly Catholic populations. And the Catholic church was against the death penalty because it was Irish and

EXECUTION METHODS BY STATE—1984

Method	States that use method
Electrocution	Alabama, Arkansas,* Connecticut, Florida, Georgia, Indiana, Kentucky, Louisiana, Nebraska, Ohio, Oklahoma,** Pennsylvania, South Carolina, Tennessee, Vermont, Virginia
Lethal injection	Arkansas,* Idaho,* Illinois, Montana,* Nevada, New Jersey, New Mexico, North Carolina,* Oklahoma,** Oregon, South Dakota, Texas, Utah,* Washington,* Wyoming*
Lethal gas	Arizona, California, Colorado, Maryland, Mississippi, Missouri, North Carolina,* Wyoming*
Hanging	Delaware, Montana,* New Hampshire, Washington*
Firing squad	Idaho,* Oklahoma,** Utah*

* Provides for two methods of execution.
** Provides for three methods of execution.

Italian Catholics who constituted the majority of those executed, just as today blacks are in that unenviable position.

Executions declined dramatically, from 199 in 1935 (high due to bootlegging and the depression) to none in 1967. In addition, there were fewer admissions

ABOLITION OF THE DEATH PENALTY BY JURISDICTION IN THE UNITED STATES

Jurisdiction[a]	Period of Abolition
Michigan[b]	1846–
Rhode Island[c]	1852–
Wisconsin	1853–
Iowa	1872–1878
Maine[d]	1876–1883
Maine	1887–
Colorado	1897–1901
Kansas[e]	1907–1935
Minnesota	1911–
Washington	1913–1919
Oregon	1914–1920
North Dakota[f]	1915–
South Dakota	1915–1939
Tennessee[g]	1915–1916
Arizona	1916–1918
Missouri	1917–1919
Alaska	1957–
Hawaii	1957–
Delaware	1958–1961
Oregon	1964–
Iowa	1965–
West Virginia	1965–
Vermont[h]	1965–
New York[i]	1965–
New Mexico[j]	1969–
New Jersey[k]	1972–
California[k]	1972–

Source: "Capital Punishment 1930–1970," *National Prisoner Statistics*, except for the judicial abolitions in New Jersey and California.

to death row in the 1960s. In fact, there were so few death row inmates that they numbered less than all the executions that had occurred in the 1930s. But this changed. The number of prisoners under sentence of death increased from 219, at the end of 1960, to 608 at the end of 1970. And between the 1930s and the 1960s, appeals of the death sentence increased from 3.2 percent to 32 percent—in other words, tenfold.

Just prior to World War II, when the United States started to abandon capital punishment, executions obviously declined also. Abolitionists held that the evidence indicated the death penalty was administered in an arbitrary manner and, they also believed, with little if any deterrent results.

Note: The table includes all legislative and judicial abolitions until June 29, 1972, when the U.S. Supreme Court invalidated existing discretionary capital statutes in *Furman* v. *Georgia.*

[a] Iowa, Maine, and Oregon appear twice in the list because each has had two distinct periods of abolition.
[b] Death penalty retained for treason until 1963.
[c] Death penalty restored in 1882 for any life-term convict who commits murder.
[d] In 1837 a law was passed to provide that no condemned person could be executed until one year after sentencing and then only upon a warrant from the governor.
[e] In 1872 a law was passed similar to the 1837 Maine statute (see note d above).
[f] Death penalty retained for murder by a prisoner serving a life term for murder.
[g] Death penalty retained for rape.
[h] Death penalty retained for murder of a police officer on duty or guard or by a prisoner guilty of a prior murder, kidnapping for ransom, and killing or destruction of vital property by a group during wartime.
[i] Death penalty retained for murder of a police officer on duty, or of anyone by a prisoner under life sentence.
[i] Death penalty retained for the crime of killing police officers or prison or jail guards while in the performance of their duties, and in cases where the jury recommends the death penalty and the defendant commits a second capital felony after time for due deliberation following commission of the first capital felony.
[k] Death penalty abolished by state supreme court decision.

Tracing the history of capital punishment back to the nineteenth century reveals that its primary purpose was to protect property. In England, with the onset of the Industrial Revolution, capital crimes increased from 8 major crimes to 223 by 1819. Many of these offenses involved crimes against property. Murder was practically put in the backseat (it constituted only 5 percent of the crimes and only 10 percent of the executions). The middle class was acquiring more property (wealth), whereas the number of those with no property (the poor) was on the rise. In the nineteenth century the United States, taking its cue from England, used capital punishment to protect another kind of property: slaves. For example, North Carolina's capital crimes, listed in 1837, included: stealing slaves, inciting slaves to rebel, concealing slaves to set them free, and circulating seditious literature among slaves (second conviction). In Virginia there were five capital crimes applied to whites and seventy applied to blacks. A white person who raped a slave, or any black, was merely subject to a fine. If a slave committed rape, the penalty was death. Thus the death penalty served to protect the institution of slavery and maintain social order for the propertied people.

Today, there are myriad reasons why capital punishment is favored by the majority of our citizens and by many of our jurists and lawmakers. These include incapacitation (a dead person cannot murder), deterrence, retribution, revenge (stemming from Mosaic law), and economic advantage (it's cheaper to kill off criminals than maintain them for life). To arrive at your own decision about the morality and efficacy of capital punishment, it's necessary to learn who and what constitutes a criminal, how our court system works, and what the Supreme Court has adjudicated. And so let's proceed to the next scene: who causes crime and why.

4

WHERE DO CRIMINALS COME FROM?

The first order of business, in weighing the pros and cons of capital punishment, is to try to have some understanding of what causes people to commit crimes. We use the word "try" because there are many different and often conflicting theories propounded by behavioral scientists (sociologists, psychologists, and others), which makes it difficult to be sure of the correct one. But an understanding of why people commit crimes is important to crime prevention. If more were known about the causes of crime and of antisocial behavior, crime would probably cease to be the overwhelming and perplexing problem that it is. However, psychiatry and psychology are still somewhat in their infancy and are more subjective than hard-core physical sciences, such as chemistry.

Crime causation has been studied by criminologists and other social scientists for over a hundred years. But the result has been only a confusion of conflicting theories and conclusions. The following pages will introduce you to a few of the better-known theories of where criminals come from.

Today capital punishment in the United States pertains only to the crime of murder, and so we shall concentrate on that violent antisocial act and then look at some others as well. The first thing to realize is that most homicides bear little resemblance to the premeditated murders depicted on television, in films, or in popular mystery fiction. Most murders are unpremeditated crimes of passion arising from an atmosphere of violence.

Cities especially are hotbeds of violence. Why? The close contact of different classes of people exacerbates the contrast between rich and poor. This causes dissatisfaction that can explode into violence. Decades ago it was the immigrant Irish, Italians, and Polish who comprised the poor underclass. Today it's Hispanics and blacks, many of whom feel a sense of hopeless deprivation and believe that prejudice has led to a lack of economic opportunity.

"In addition to the sense of deprivation in the underclass, its members share with the rest of us profound changes in the routines of family life, the common loss of confidence in our public institutions, and the erosion of religious authority." This combination of negatives, Professor John P. Conrad states, in the book *The Death Penalty: A Debate,* is a potent cause of crime. While conservative behavioral scientists deny the notion that poverty and deprivation

Supporters of the electric chair, a device developed in the late nineteenth century, defended its use as a humane instrument of execution.

have anything to do with crime, Conrad believes this "flies in the face of realties that they can see for themselves in New York—and I can see for myself in Los Angeles and San Francisco."

The above is one point of view. But then there's Professor Ernest van den Haag, on the conservative side of the sociological fence, who asks, Why does the United States have such a comparatively high crime rate compared to other affluent countries—Japan, France, and Germany? One explanation offered by those who disagree with him is that there is far greater homogeneity of nationality and race in those countries. In *The Death Penalty: A Debate,* Van den Haag states: "Currently we make crime (and welfare) pay. And then lament that there is so much of it . . . or we take seriously . . . [that it is] really the fault of society, criminals are not to blame, and more employment would solve the problem. When we had practically no unemployment our crime rates did not fall."

Van den Haag's statements represent an ultra-conservative attitude and in some instances his statistical analyses are considered questionable by many other social scientists. Nevertheless, his ideas represent one point of view as to where criminals come from and how to deter crime.

A more humanitarian viewpoint is expressed in *Crime and Human Nature* by two Harvard professors, James Q. Wilson and Richard J. Hernstein. There is some evidence, they believe, that criminal tendencies can be inherited. They base this theory on such data as the following: identical twins resemble each other more closely in their crime rate than do fraternal twins, and adopted children resemble their biological parents more than they do the foster parents who raised them. This would seem to show that poverty and unemployment are not the sole causes of crime. On the other hand, the authors point out that street crimes are far more numerous among the lower socio-economic classes. This applies, too, to those who commit violent crimes (rape and assault), whose anti-social behavior is obviously not for the sake of obtaining money. Also, criminals appear to have a lower verbal IQ than the average person.

In trying to further explore why certain groups of criminals commit crimes, the authors present this proposition: a person is likely to commit a crime if it seems that the total rewards, discounted by the delay in their attainment, are greater than the total disadvantages. In other words, if the "pleasure" resulting from such violent behavior as venting momentary rage or stealing money is almost instantaneous, this makes the crime worthwhile. Since punishments for the crime—if discovered—are events that only happen later, these negatives can be disregarded.

What about conscience—which is generally conceded to be an important factor in restraining criminal actions? Is it lacking in criminals, and if so why? Obviously it is, or they would not opt to be criminals. But why this lack? The authors point out that if, in their first three and a half years, children lack a secure attachment to parents or foster parents or parent figures, the children will grow up not caring for anyone's approval and with no sense of guilt (that is, conscience). Furthermore, if children are either unjustly punished or not punished at all, or are not rewarded for good behavior, they are very apt to do as they please. Thus, the urge for instant gratification, with little or no regard for possible future punishment, encourages them to commit crimes. Conversely, children with good familial relationships are likely to be able to wait for rewards and fear punishment in case of bad behavior. Finally, according to Wilson and Hernstein, there seem to be three strong factors that can twist human beings into criminals—inherited

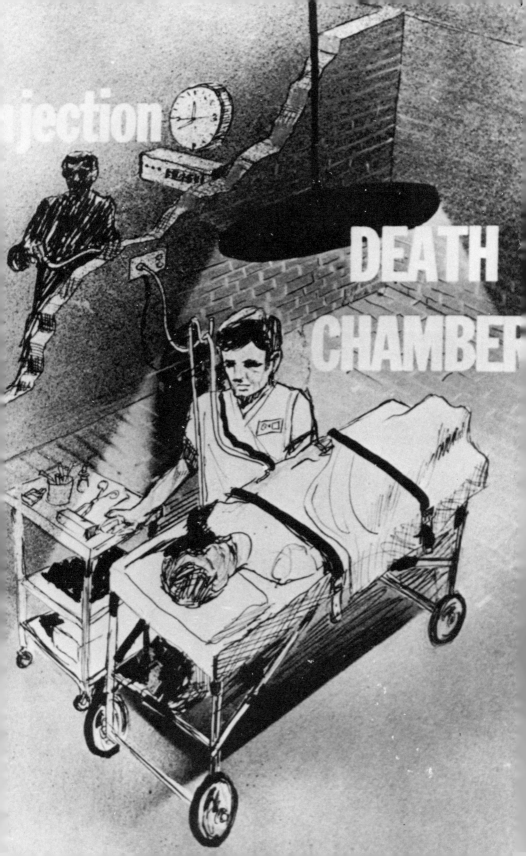

traits, family environment, and, never to be disregarded, school and peer pressures, as well as neighhood environment.

If you're somewhat confused about what causes criminal behavior, it's because there are so many different theories. Let's boil them down to some concrete examples. There is little doubt that some people who commit major crimes suffer from serious psychological disturbances—a factor we have not touched upon. But even those who commit murder are not necessarily sick or affected by social pressures. There is ample sociological evidence that shows that some forms of murder can be due to primitive values and abnormal behavior and to special situational factors. To illustrate what this means: Most people believe that incest is the result of mental illness. Yet studies clearly reveal that it is partly attributable to sociological conditions—unavailability of more appropriate sexual partners, due to illness of the spouse; social and physical isolation of the family unit; covert collaboration by the spouse.

As another example: It's usually believed that kleptomania (an impulse to steal without financial motive) is a "compulsive" crime—a sickness. However, studies show that the term *kleptomania* is a euphemism applied to "nice people" (the affluent)

Some states consider death by lethal injection a more humane technique than electrocution. This drawing demonstrates the method. The prisoner is prepared for the injection in the death chamber. When ready, a person in another room starts the lethal flow.

who steal and not to "bad people" (the poor) who are branded crooks and thieves.

There are, to be sure, those whose behavior seems to be the result of psychological problems. But because the mass news media usually play up crimes of violence, the public has a distorted view of crime. In fact, for every lurid crime committed, there are thousands of petty thefts, well-planned burglaries, professional swindles and white-collar crimes—none of which stem from mental illness. Crimes of violence are far less frequent than property offenses. Furthermore, many acts of criminal violence are impulsive and not repetitive. Abysmal social conditions are often the basis of antisocial outlooks and behavior especially in the inner cities where unemployment among teenagers is as high as 40 percent, and where the rate of unemployment among blacks and Hispanics is double that among whites. "Taking up a criminal 'occupation' may be an almost rational decision given the nature of the available alternatives, and the prevalence of numerous acts that are at least technically criminal among otherwise 'respectable' citizens, [makes it] quite absurd to insist on the basic psychopathology of *most* American crime. Indeed, the only way in which such a claim could be substantiated would be as a corollary to a more general assertion that most if not all Americans are mentally ill."

So states sociology professor Edwin M. Schur, who believes that there is no definitive answer to the question of what causes criminal behavior. Research is still inadequate and it is unlikely that one will ever be able to measure a person's "criminal tendencies," if such a thing exists at all. The complexity of various types of crime, coupled with the fact that what is criminal is often subject to variation, makes the attempt to find an answer even more complicated. Large-scale studies have led many sociologists to believe that the

*Maximum-security prisons
isolate criminals from society.*

tendency toward violence in an individual is learned in specific social contexts, varies according to social status, and is in large measure a response to pressures generated by particular special conditions. Furthermore, one should be aware of the fact that our criminal law represents, in some respects, the efforts of the middle and upper classes to control the working and lower classes; of whites to control blacks; of men to control women; of adults to control youth.

There's another type of criminal who receives far too little attention: a corporation. Its crimes are not only endemic to our society, but alarmingly on the increase. They range from chicanery and thievery to murder, including mass murder. To cite just a few examples: E. F. Hutton Company, one of the country's largest brokerage firms, was cited for kiting (falsifying balances of) millions of dollars but was little more than chastised. Exxon was fined $2 billion for bilking consumers (that's us), but no individual member of the corporation paid a price for this and the fine was merely a corporate tax write-off. Eli Lilly, one of the nation's leading pharmaceutical firms, pleaded guilty to twenty-five counts of failing to inform the government of the possibly fatal effects of its drug, Oraflex, which in some instances did occur. The deaths it caused amounted to inadvertent murder. A. H. Robins's Dalkon Shield (a contraceptive device used by millions of women) was responsible for thousands of seriously injured women and over fifteen deaths in the United States alone. The Ford Motor Company has been charged with continuing to sell Pintos even though these cars could explode when hit in the rear. Why? It was said that a study showed it was cheaper to pay off for dead and injured consumers than to change the cars.

What kinds of penalties were imposed for crimes that were tantamount to murder? You can't hang, electrocute, gas, or shoot a corporation. What about corporate officials? As one attorney put it: "No one man is responsible—there are committees, boards, panels. It becomes the thinking of a corporation, not an individual." Thus corporate crime seems practically immune to punishment, despite the fact that it can directly and indirectly affect all of us. This kind of designed neglect of corporate malfeasance could benefit from the studies and guidance of social scientists, too. Criminologists could perform a useful service by showing how the stresses of corporate life can transform some individuals into tools of corporate greed.

5

ARE THE SCALES OF JUSTICE LOADED?

If the scales of our justice system were guaranteed to always be in balance, one argument against capital punishment would be destroyed. If a person is sentenced to a prison term and subsequently found not guilty, that person can be released and economic restitution made. Even though this is scant compensation for the time robbed from one's life, and no mitigation for the humiliation and trauma of incarceration, at least justice would have prevailed. On the other hand, if that person had been electrocuted, shot, gassed, hanged, or intravenously poisoned, there would scarcely be a comforting way to say, "Sorry about that, you're innocent and may go free." The dead are exceptionally hard of hearing.

Roy Calvert, a leading English opponent of capital punishment, noted in his book *Capital Punishment in the Twentieth Century* (published in 1927), "The fact that few errors of justice come to light in connection with capital offenses should not lead us to suppose that such mistakes do not occur." But this argument against capital punishment can not really be tested. It is as weak as a retentionist's (one who wants capital punishment retained) statement that capital punishment serves as a deterrent, even though few cases of deterrence have as yet been verified. Facts, not wishful thinking or opinions, should decide the issue.

In what way, if any, are our scales of justice loaded? In one study, reported in *The Death Penalty in America* by Hugo A. Bedau, murder cases were carefully analyzed and it was subsequently proved that from 1893 to 1962 there were seventy-four instances of faulty convictions. The study results are as follows:

Death sentence executed	8
Death sentence not executed	23
Life sentence	30
Less than life sentence	10
Convictions averted	3
Total	74

Bedau, the criminologist who made this study, comments that it is surprising, to say the least, that of seven thousand people executed during the period, only eight probably "erroneous executions and an additional twenty-three erroneous death sentences have been discovered."

He used the word "discovered," implying that there could be many more such miscarriages of justice. But uncovering them depends largely on tireless investigation and persistence in persuading those responsible to admit their error. Furthermore, it is fair to assume that there have been instances in which poverty, fear, or lack of ingenuity allowed for judicial errors in homicide convictions "to go unchallenged, unproved, or uncorrected."

Bedau's study adds that once people are found guilty, they cannot easily have their innocence established without cooperation from the prosecuting attorneys who convicted them. In every case investigated, the prosecutor's office was as uncooperative as possible. This is understandable if one is aware of the instances of forced confessions, denials of counsel, subornation (inducing) of perjury, withheld evidence, and racially biased juries, which were shown to have been involved in the seventy-four cases of faulty convictions.

Juries and judges, too, can be and have been influenced by prejudices—the most potent one being racial. A racially biased justice system means that the scales are loaded against the accused black or Hispanic. If this is the case, it creates a strong argument against capital punishment, where judicial malfunctions cannot be reversed. What are the facts?

In 1935 more people were executed—199—than in any other year in our history. The statistics for that year, says Dr. Bedau, in *The Courts, the Constitution, and Capital Punishment,* are typical: 3 females; more whites (119) than blacks, but the proportion of blacks far exceeded that in the general population. Between 1930 and 1966, half of those executed were black. Blacks comprised approximately 12 percent of the population, yet 50 percent of those executed were black. Was this the result of bias or of a far higher crime rate for blacks? The evidence points to bias. For example, in Virginia there were 56 executions of blacks for rape and none for whites. A study in New Jersey similarly showed that blacks charged with first-degree murder were given harsher sentences.

The following chart demonstrates what appears to be racially slanted justice, for out of 50 executed, 17 (34 percent) were black:

EXECUTIONS—1977–1985

Date	Defendant	State	Race	Race of Victim(s)
1/17/77	*Gary Gilmore	UT	W	W
5/25/79	John Spenkelink	FL	W	W
10/22/79	*Jesse Bishop	NV	W	W
3/9/81	*Steven Judy	IN	W	W
8/10/82	*Frank Coppola	VA	W	W
12/7/82	Charlie Brooks	TX	B	W
4/22/83	John Evans	AL	W	W
9/2/83	Jimmy Lee Gray	MS	W	W
11/30/83	Robert Sullivan	FL	W	W
12/14/83	Robert Wayne Williams	LA	B	B
12/15/83	John Eldon Smith	GA	W	W
1/26/84	Anthony Antone	FL	W	W
2/29/84	John Taylor	LA	B	W
3/14/84	James Autry	TX	W	W
3/16/84	James Hutchins	NC	W	W
3/31/84	Ronald O'Bryan	TX	W	W
4/5/84	Arthur Goode	FL	W	W
4/5/84	Elmo Sonnier	LA	W	W
5/10/84	James Adams	FL	B	W
6/20/84	Carl Shriner	FL	W	W
7/12/84	Ivon Stanley	GA	B	W
7/13/84	David Washington	FL	B	W/B
9/7/84	Ernest Dobbert	FL	W	W
9/10/84	Timothy Baldwin	LA	W	W
9/20/84	James Henry	FL	B	B
10/12/84	Linwood Briley	VA	B	W
10/30/84	Thomas Barefoot	TX	W	W
10/30/84	Ernest Knighton	LA	B	W
11/2/84	Velma Barfield	NC	W	W
11/8/84	Timothy Palmes	FL	W	W
12/12/84	Alpha Otis Stephens	GA	B	W

Date	Defendant	State	Race	Race of Victim(s)
12/28/84	Robert Lee Willie	LA	W	W
1/4/85	David Martin	LA	W	W
1/9/85	Roosevelt Green	GA	B	W
1/11/85	Joseph Carl Shaw	SC	W	W
1/16/85	Doyle Skillern	TX	W	W
1/30/85	James Raulerson	FL	W	W
2/20/85	Van Roosevelt Solomon	GA	B	W
3/6/85	Johnny Paul Witt	FL	W	W
3/13/85	*Stephen Peter Morin	TX	W	W
3/20/85	John Young	GA	B	W
4/18/85	James Briley	VA	B	B
5/15/85	Jesse de la Rosa	TX	H	W
5/29/85	Marvin Francois	FL	B	B
6/25/85	Charles Milton	TX	B	B
6/25/85	Morris Mason	VA	B	W
7/9/85	Henry Martinez Porter	TX	H	W
9/11/85	*Charles Rumbaugh	TX	W	W
10/16/85	*William Vandiver	IN	W	W
12/6/85	*Carroll Cole	NV	W	U

Source: NAACP Legal Defense and Educational Fund.

* Voluntary

There are additional ways, too, in which the scales of justice lose their equilibrium. Lack of funds is one. As an example: In New Jersey in 1960 three men were to be executed just after Easter. They were poor and had no funds to hire attorneys to postpone their executions by the necessary legal means. Then a miracle occurred—at the last moment voluntary legal aid came to their rescue. Two years later one conviction was *reversed,* and the other two men were still alive pending further legal action. On the other hand, as pointed out in *The Death Penalty in America,* "it is difficult to find cases where persons of means or social position have been executed. The wealthy al-

Cell blocks such as this one hold over 1,600 prisoners now on death row.

ways have been able to hire expert legal counsel and thus have been almost certain to avoid the death penalty."

There is still another way that the scales of justice can be tipped in favor of the prosecution: by the testimony of psychologists or psychiatrists. Their judgments may not necessarily be based upon facts, but upon opinions. In one instance two such experts, after an hour interview each, were positive that the defendant knew the difference between right and wrong and that he was a threat to society. Thus, he could not plead insanity although these psychologists also knew that he had lived his life in an abnormal way.

To illustrate further oddities of justice: In December 1982, Charles Brooks, Jr., was executed by lethal injection in Texas. His accomplice, Woody Loudres, pleaded guilty at his second trial and got forty years, with a possible parole in six, even though *he committed the same crime!*

In his book *Capital Punishment,* Professor Charles L. Black, Jr., analyzes the probability of errors relating to charges of murder. He lists three basic areas where errors can occur.

THE PROSECUTOR

Based on the facts presented, the prosecutor must decide whether to charge the suspect with an offense. Assuming the accused has been charged with a capital offense, the prosecutor often has to decide whether to accept a plea of guilty to a lesser offense instead. This permits the defendant to avoid possible execution in exchange for going to prison without trial. In some instances the prosecutor makes the decision in cooperation with a grand jury. But usually the grand jury relies heavily on the prosecutor's opinion. Since prosecutors are no more immune to human fallibility than others, the possibility of error lurks in this first step.

THE DEFENSE LAWYER

When the prosecutor charges a defendant with a capital offense but is willing to accept a plea of guilty to a lesser offense, the defendant, theoretically, has the option of accepting or rejecting the alternative. However, the accused is more than likely in a state of emotional turmoil, frightened and confused and, consequently, relies upon the advice of a lawyer. Here is where another error in judgment can occur. For example, some defendants may, in fact, not be guilty, but the defense lawyers may nevertheless advise them to plead guilty to lesser offenses in order to avoid trial, the risk of conviction, and the possibility of execution. Should the defendants elect to stand trial, their fate is completely in the hands of their defense attorneys. If the criminal lawyers are skilled, whether the accused are guilty or not, the chances of acquittal are good. If not, however, the outcome may be fatal—a tragedy for an innocent person.

THE JURY

The defendant's fate is also in the hands of the jurors. Here, too, human fallibility can enter the picture. In fact, more so. At the end of the trial the jurors are faced with a number of decisions to make, each of which can be subject to error. To illustrate this: Did the defendant stab the victim or did someone else? Did the defendant commit the murder while or because the victim was trying to stab the accused, or did the defendant stab the victim while the murdered person's knife was still sheathed? These are examples of the *physical facts* on which a jury must decide. But

*The accused prisoner—frightened and surrounded
by guards and police officers—must rely upon
the advice of an unknown defense lawyer.*

Jurors in a murder trial are escorted from the court to a motel in which they will live for the duration of the trial so that they will not be influenced by press coverage or public opinion.

then there are far more tenuous *psychological factors.* Let us suppose that the defendant clearly, or admittedly, shot a man while the victim was reaching for his handkerchief. This poses a number of questions. Did the defendant believe that the man was actually reaching for a gun, or was that a lie? Or, did the accused plan the killing or was it committed in a state of violent anger? Did the defendant intend to kill at all? Were there any extenuating circumstances that caused the killing? Because of the difficulties jurors are faced with, they sometimes find a defendant guilty of second-degree rather than first-degree murder when they are in doubt. Thus it is the jurors' choice to decide whether a defendant should be put to death or not.

To further complicate their ability to make a decision, there is the question of the defendant's sanity. Prior to trial a court may have to decide whether the accused is sane enough to be tried. If the answer is affirmative, the twelve jurors must decide whether the defendant was sane at the time the crime was committed. Since psychiatrists themselves often differ on the definition of sanity, where does that leave the jurors? Confused.

"The jury," Professor Black states, "is also called upon to pronounce upon mixed questions of fact and law, questions that have puzzled the most astute legal minds." Legal jargon is often obscure even for the trained professional. Where does that leave the juror? Additionally confused. And presiding judges seldom try to clarify matters for the jurors. Where does all this leave our system of justice? Often confused and lopsided.

And where does this leave the question of capital punishment? Mined with the possibility that an innocent person will be executed.

6

PROS AND CONS OF THE DEATH PENALTY

In order to justify capital punishment, the prime consideration is its effectiveness as a deterrent. If it doesn't reduce crime, it can only be justified on the grounds that it is the most economical way to remove a dangerous criminal from society. Or that executing someone for murder or treason is proper societal retribution.

To sanction the death penalty for economic reasons means equating the value of human life with money. That's tantamount to killing for the sake of economy. To justify it on the principle of "an eye for an eye" is contrary to any strivings for humanitarian principles. Thus the number one consideration is whether capital punishment does reduce the incidence of crime.

That sounds simple enough—but it's far from it. Because, to date, there is no irrefutable evidence to prove that the death penalty is a deterrent to crime. There is more data showing that it is not. There are

SUPPORT THE DEATH
PENALTY THE LIFE YOU
SAVE MAY BE YOUR OWN
GET THE WORMS OUT
OF THE BIG APPLE
VOTE FOR THE
DEATH PENALTY
GOV CUOMO
U TIE THE HANDS
OF THOSE WE HI
TO ENFORCE THE
LAW
LIFE IMPRISONMENT
PACIFIES-BUT THE
DEATH PENALTY
WILL FINALIZE

several reasons why there is no absolute proof. First, there are so many variables involved. The probability of receiving the death penalty may depend upon the possible offender's age, education, income, social status, sex, occupation, marital status, and the average probability of receiving the death penalty in the given society. Further, the governments of Canada and Great Britain have spent large sums on research to arrive at a decision regarding the efficacy of the death penalty prior to abolishing capital punishment. Our government has not. Thus we have not tried to gather sufficient data in order to arrive at an intelligent conclusion.

To help you come to a decision about capital punishment, let's examine some of the pro arguments first. Its leading protagonist and spokesperson is Professor Ernest van den Haag. Here, in part, is how he expressed himself as a proponent of capital punishment in the *New York Times* on October 17, 1983:

> Arguments for and against the death penalty are either moral or utilitarian. Morally, I believe that anyone who takes another's life should not be encouraged to expect that he will outlive his victim at public expense. Murder must forfeit the murderer's life if there is to be justice.

Death-penalty proponents bring their cause to the New York State Capitol in 1985. They called for support of the death penalty instead of a proposed sentence of life without parole.

Abolitionists disagree, believing that society has no right to take the life even of a murderer. . . . Variations of the abolitionist moral argument suggest that the death penalty may be applied discriminatorily and disproportionately or that innocents may be executed . . . the discrimination and mistake arguments are a sham. . . . Common sense, lately bolstered by statistics, tells us that that the death penalty will deter murder, if anything can. People fear nothing more than death. . . . Death is final. But where there's life there's hope. Therefore life in prison is less feared. . . . I have occasionally asked abolitionists if they would favor the death penalty were it shown that every execution deters, say, 500 murders. The answer to this admittedly hypothetical question, after some dodging, has always been no. . . . this demonstrates that abolitionists want to abolish the death penalty regardless of whether it deters. . . . It is fair to conclude that they would rather save the life of a convicted murderer than that of any number of innocent victims.

There are a number of additional arguments Van den Haag offers. He says that all of us are condemned to death at some time and an execution is often less painful than wasting away with cancer or another fatal disease. The belief that some commit murder as a devious form of suicide by state execution he refutes as follows: One might just as well suggest that high buildings be abolished as they are tempting to would-be suicides. Van den Haag does firmly believe that preexecution cruelties (such as tiny cells and extremely restricted activities) as well as prolonged delays of the execution dates should be abolished.

And that the killing should be as painless as possible. If there is no proof that the death penalty fails to deter, he believes, why not use it and thus protect the innocent from possible murder?

In zeroing in on "the lack of proof that the death penalty does not deter," Van den Haag sums up his position thus: "Unfortunately, there is little proof of the sort sought by those who oppose the death penalty, for the deterrent effect of any sort of punishment. Nobody has statistics showing that four years in prison deter more than two, or twenty more than ten. We assume as much. But I know of no statistical proof. One may wonder why such proof is demanded for the death penalty but not for any other. To be sure, death is more serious a punishment than any other. But ten years in prison are not exactly trivial either."

Judges, Van den Haag claims, dislike the death penalty far more than the general public. Why? "They are college educated. Usually they were told by their professors that the death penalty is cruel and obsolete." The reasons, he says, that the majority of college-educated people are abolitionists, whereas the less-educated majority are not, are twofold. First, the more educated, including judges, are most unlikely to live in an environment where violence, including murder, is a daily threat. Therefore, not feeling threatened, they can afford humanitarian sentiments. The less-educated and poorer people who live in that environment cannot afford such "sentimentality." Second, college education may have some advantages but it has this disadvantage: "Students tend to absorb and to be victimized by the intellectual fashions of their college days. . . . the idea of the criminal as a sick victim of society thrives among intellectuals."

Let us now hear from the con side, first with Professor John P. Conrad's refutation of the last assertion about the attitude of the educated classes. In England abolition of the death penalty occurred when the Labour party was in office in 1965, and in France abolition of the death penalty "was hardly considered until 1981, when a socialist government took office. In both nations, opposition to the death penalty was a predilection of the working classes, the plain people on whose common sense and perception of the realities of violence Professor van den Haag sets such great store."

The following data also seems to refute Van den Haag's contention that the more educated were against the death penalty and the less educated were for it:

GALLUP POLL (JAN. 11–14, 1985)

	Favoring Death Penalty	Opposing Death Penalty	No opinion
College graduates	74%	18%	7%
Some college	76	16	8
High school graduates	75	19	6
Less than high school graduates	65	23	12

From the ethical aspect, here is a sampling of opinions from some of our leading jurists and intellectuals. Supreme Court justice Louis D. Brandeis once said,

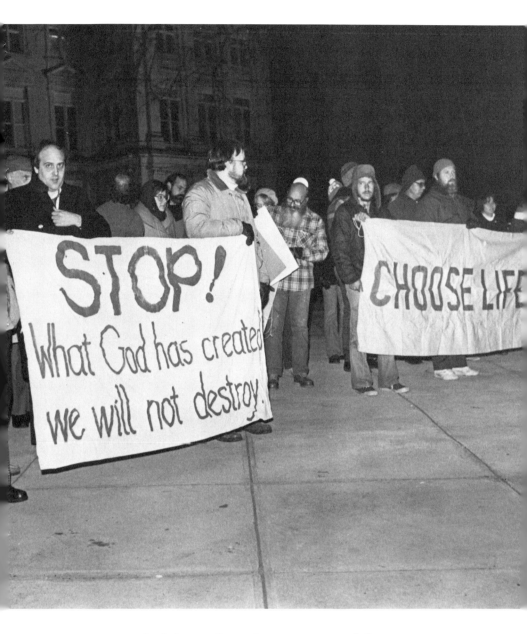

In Atlanta, Georgia, opponents of the death penalty protest an electrocution.

*In Carson City, Nevada, protestors hold a
candlelight vigil before an execution.*

"Inevitably, the state is a teacher and when it kills, it teaches vengeance and hatred."

The legal philosopher H. L. A. Hart offered three main arguments against capital punishment:

1. To take any life is to impose suffering not only on the criminal but also on many others—an evil that can be justified only if some good end is achieved thereby that could not be achieved by any other means.

2. Although the danger is small, the death penalty cannot be expunged if it is discovered that an innocent person has been executed—an intolerable risk.

3. The nature of the death penalty distorts the entire criminal justice system. Trials become interminable and in spite of all precautions, elaborate appellate processes preoccupy the courts at vast expense not only of money, but also of public confidence in the judicial process. Protracted waiting for death mocks the fundamental purpose of justice, the swift and sure imposition of the penalty for the crime.

Former United States attorney general Ramsey Clark stated before a Senate subcommittee: "Society pays a heavy price for the penalty of death it imposes. Our emotions may cry vengeance in the wake of a horrible crime. But reason and experience tell us that killing the criminal will not undo the crime, prevent other crimes, or bring justice to the victim, the criminal, or society. Executions cheapen life. We must cherish life. . . . The death penalty should be abolished."

To go from what some might consider the tenuous to the more tangible: Does the death penalty deter? Hugo A. Bedau, in his book *The Courts, the Constitution, and Capital Punishment,* says: "Van den Haag is correct in affirming that deterrence has not been determined statistically, but he is incorrect in denying that nondeterrence has been demonstrated statistically: his suggestion that the added severity of the death penalty contributes to its deterrent function, is unempirical and one-sided as well; finally, his contention regarding the burden of proof which he would impose entirely upon abolitionists, is a dodge and is based on a muddled analysis."

According to Professor Kilman Shin in *Death Penalty and Crime:* "Assuming that the deterrence should be most in evidence in days immediately following the execution and in the locality where the crimes are committed and the criminals are known, [researchers] observed the murder rates of Philadelphia for 60 days before and after the highly publicized executions of Philadelphia murderers in 1927, '29, '30 and '32, and found no deterrence effect . . . there were 91 murders in the before-execution periods, and 113 in the after-execution periods. . . . [Researchers compared] the murder rates in Philadelphia for eight weeks before and after the death sentence was imposed for four highly publicized cases in 1944, '46, '47, and found no deterrence effect . . . first degree murder increased from 23 to 28 . . . there emerges no pattern that would indicate deterrence."

Shin concludes by saying: "One may or may not argue against or for the death penalty. However, such argument may be based on one's own moral value judgment, and the deterrence theory is apparently without any conclusive evidence."

In a study of the deterrence effect of the death penalty on prisoners, Professor Bedau states: "It may come as somewhat of a shock to learn that research published during recent years shows convincingly that the rate of assaults, fatal or otherwise, in prisons by prisoners bears no correlation whatever to the severity of the punishment for such crimes. Prisoners in death-penalty states are as likely, or more likely, to commit such crimes as are convicts in abolition

Anti-death penalty protestors demonstrate outside a Florida prison.

states." Bedau adds that there is no evidence that the death penalty serves as protection for the police, but that police run no higher risk in abolition states than they do in death-penalty jurisdictions.

In testifying before the House Subcommittee on the Judiciary, the criminologist Professor Marvin E. Wolfgang stated that a study of homicide rates four years prior to 1967 (when executions were suspended) and four years afterward shows the criminal homicide rate increased at a slower pace than any of the other major crimes in the *Uniform Crime Reports* of the FBI. For all serious crimes (homicide, rape, robbery, aggravated assaults and battery, burglary, larceny, auto theft), there was a 42.6 percent increase between 1967 and 1970, but only a 27.8 percent increase for criminal homicide, and the increase in the homicide rate from 1963 to 1967 was 35.5 percent while the increase from 1967–1970 was only 27.8 percent.

Canada abolished the death penalty in 1976. But prior to that, from 1962 to 1976, no one was executed. In that period the murder rate remained stable, and from 1976 to 1980 (from abolition on), as the following table shows, there was a decline in the incidence of murder. The average murder rate for the last five years (to 1980) was 2.87 per 100,000 as compared with a rate of 8.49 per 100,000 in the United States.

"No doubt," Professor Conrad states, "some retentionists will patiently explain to me that Canada is very different from the United States. Smaller population. Much more homogeneous. No large racial minorities. All these and more quibbles can be freely granted . . . [nevertheless] I do not see any challenge that obviates a declining homicide rate in the face of nationwide abolition of capital punishment that has been in effect for six years."

NUMBER AND RATE (PER 100,000 POPULATION) MURDER INCIDENTS, CANADA, 1961–1980

Year	Murder incidents	Rate
1961	172	0.94
1962	196	1.05
1963	192	1.01
1964	199	1.03
1965	216	1.10
1966	206	1.03
1967	239	1.17
1968	292	1.41
1969	320	1.52
1970	354	1.66
1971	395	1.83
1972	414	1.90
1973	448	2.03
1974	500	2.23
1975	569	2.50
1976	561	2.43
1977	575	2.47
1970	554	2.36
1979	537	2.27
1980	459	1.92

Source: Canadian Center for Justice Statistics.

We could cite more statistics that would provide further evidence, for those opposing the death penalty, that abolition of capital punishment does not increase the incidence of murder, and that the retention of the death penalty does not decrease it. However, such data is not yet final. As Professor Bedau frankly states, "The argument against capital punishment and in favor of abolition is by no means conclusively established." However, based upon the limited current data, there is good reason to believe that the death penalty does not deter.

7
CAPITAL PUNISHMENT, THE SUPREME COURT, AND CONFUSION

The United States Supreme Court is the highest court in our judicial system. For better or for worse, its decisions are the final word. Its nine justices are political appointees, which may explain why some of them have not been paragons of judicial wisdom. They are selected by the president (when a vacancy occurs) subject to the approval of the Senate. Judging from the past, a liberal president is apt to select a jurist who has manifested liberal tendencies and a conservative president is apt to select a conservative-minded jurist. It should be apparent, therefore, that these justices are not superbeings but human beings. They have been and are subject to prejudices—political and ideological—in short, and understandably, to human fallibility.

Consequently, it should come as no surprise that this "last bastion for the protection of people's rights" has sometimes deemed property rights more important than people's rights, as the Court's past record shows. For example, in the *Dred Scott* decision, the Court ruled that the Constitution considered a slave the property of the owner and thus "property" had no right to sue its owner. In the 1880s and 1890s the Court ruled in a number of cases that state segregation laws did not violate the Fourteenth Amendment. However, on numerous other occasions the Court has rendered decisions that have protected the rights of individuals against encroachment by the state.

In evaluating the pros and cons of capital punishment, it's important that you are aware of the paradoxical nature of the Court: its potential for fallibility in some instances in contrast to the fairness and wisdom it has demonstrated on other occasions. In some instances the Court has been swayed by public opinion; at other times it has maintained its independence and objectivity. Justice Thurgood Marshall, in commenting on a poll showing that the public favored the death penalty two to one, said that public opinion is only relevant to interpreting the Constitution when it's "informed" opinion.

It is generally accepted that the Supreme Court's basic function is to make certain that the legislative and executive branches of our government adhere to the tenets of the Constitution. However, Professor Raoul Berger states that "the track record of the Court does not inspire confidence that it is a better judge of what the people should do than the people themselves."

Commenting on a study released in 1985 which asserts that in the twentieth century 343 people have been wrongfully convicted of capital offenses and that 25 have been executed, Henry Schwarzschild, director of the American Civil Liberties Union's capital punishment project said: "The study shows that in hundreds of routine criminal cases, including cases where the defendant's life is at stake, the criminal justice system makes egregious errors. It convicts innocent people and it executes innocent people."

Whether the above criticisms are justified or not, the Court seems to be the final arbiter of the issue of capital punishment, which is why it's important to learn about some of the justices' opinions on the subject. In 1972 the Supreme Court, for the first time, issued a ruling about the death penalty in its *Furman* v. *Georgia* decision. Headlines at the time of the decision screamed that the Court had virtually banned capital punishment. As is patently evident, this was far from factual. Legal scholars at the time correctly predicted that state legislatures *could* write capital punishment laws that would remove certain objections and pass the test of constitutionality. In four years' time, by 1976, thirty-five states had already enacted new legislation tailored to meet the objections cited in *Furman* v. *Georgia*.

The *Furman* decision far from settled the question of capital punishment. If anything it added to the confusion. Eight of the nine justices revealed that they were personally against the death penalty, but only five agreed that the death penalty, as then administered, violated the Constitution and only two of the justices maintained that the death penalty violated the Constitution in any form. The *Furman* decision centered on what constitutes "cruel and unusual punishment" within the meaning of the Eighth Amendment as applied to the state (in this case Georgia) by the Fourteenth Amendment.

Justice Douglas, in his concurring statement, wrote: "I vote to vacate each judgment, believing that the action of the death penalty does violate the Eighth and Fourteenth Amendments."

Among the reasons he cited was the following: "The President's Commission on Law Enforcement and Administration of Justice recently concluded:

Ronald Reagan, then Governor of California,
opposed the abolition of the death penalty.
In 1972 the State Supreme Court struck
down the death penalty in the state.

'Finally: there is evidence that the imposition of the death sentence and the exercise of dispensing power by the courts and the executive follow discriminatory patterns. The death sentence is disproportionately imposed and carried out on the poor, the Negro, and the members of unpopular groups.' "

The chart on page 52 seems to give substance to the charges of bias. The chart below, showing individuals on death row, as of December 1985, provides additional evidence:

Race	Number	Percent
White	836	50.91
Black	678	41.30
Hispanic	97	5.91
Native American	21	1.28
Asian	5	.30
Unknown	5	.30

Source: NAACP Legal Defense
and Educational Fund.

The dissenting justices, for their part, stated, "The Court rejects as not decisive the clearest evidence that the Framers of the Constitution and the authors of the Fourteenth Amendment believed that those documents posed no barrier to the death penalty."

Professor Berger, in his criticism of the Court's decisions in his book, *Death Penalties,* insists that just because blacks are sentenced to death for murder and whites are not, for the identical crime, does not authorize the Court to abolish the death penalty on constitutional grounds. According to Berger, the Supreme Court has no right to interpret at will the Constitution and change the meaning of various amendments. Berger believes that such amendments should remain as they were intended and not be updated by the justices, because "this search for a social consensus (as Justices Warren and Frankfurter suggested) amounts to double talk for amending the Constitution without consulting the people."

Berger further maintains that the Court's death-penalty decision was tampering with and curbing jury discretion in sentencing. "[This] has even less constitutional footing and already has resulted in a quagmire of contradictions. It is not alone that there was no judicial assertion of such power prior to 1972, but that the Court has invaded the constitutional province of the jury."

Berger argues that the Founders made clear their preference for the common-law mode of trial by jury: juries could not be challenged to explain their verdicts nor did judges have the power to review verdicts. "If the Court is free to substitute its own meaning for the established common law content of the constitutional terms, it obliterates those limits and revises the Constitution for the imposition of its own predilections on a people who, in the case of death penalties, lost no time in repudiating the Court's reading of prevailing standards of human decency."

Berger also quotes Justice John Harlan, who supported his stance: " 'When the Court disregards the express intent and understanding of the Framers, it has invaded the realm of the political process to which the amending power was committed, and it has violated the constitutional structure which it is its highest duty to protect.' "

It should be pointed out that trial by one's peers—the jury system—has sometimes caricactured American justice. Consider this example: In 1978 Dan White entered San Francisco's City Hall and deliberately shot and killed Mayor George Moscone and then proceeded to another office and shot and killed Harvey

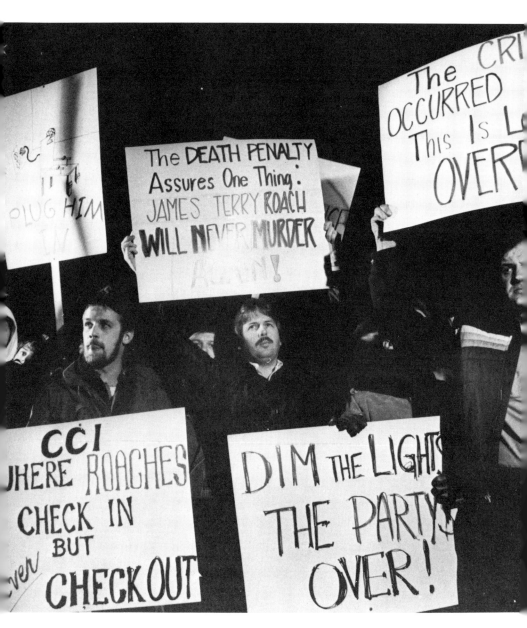

Death-penalty supporters demonstrate their approval of a 1986 execution.

Protestors march to present their views opposing capital punishment.

Milk, a town supervisor who ran for public office openly acknowledging that he was homosexual. White enjoyed a jury of his peers—all white, gays excluded —who, despite evidence that the murders were premeditated, rendered a verdict of manslaughter. Dan White was freed on parole after serving five and a half years. He later committed suicide.

After the *Furman* decision the Court issued many additional ones. None of these decisions clarified, but rather seemed to add to the confusion around the issue. The lack of consensus among the justices resulted in death-penalty inequities. The intent of the subsequent decisions was to remove arbitrariness and ensure evenhandedness in applying capital punishment—not to abolish the death penalty—but they had little success. In the *Gregg* v. *Georgia* decision (seven–two), the majority opinion stated, "We now hold that the punishment of death does not inevitably violate the Constitution." The Court's decisions also seemed to indicate that in those jurisdictions where there was capital punishment, the death penalty was not always equitably applied. For example: Gregg, a hitchhiker, robbed and killed the two men who gave him a ride, and he was sentenced to death. The Court upheld the verdict. In North Carolina, Woodson, who had robbed and killed a storekeeper and was sentenced to death by a lower court, had his sentence overturned (*Woodson* v. *North Carolina*) by the Supreme Court! Because of the differences of the death-penalty laws in the two states (Georgia and North Carolina), the Court ruled differently—upholding one verdict, but not the other. The end result is difficult to comprehend.

Inequity does not stop there. In the case of *Lockett* v. *Ohio* (1978), Lockett had been the driver of the getaway car in the robbery and murder of a pawnbroker. Under Ohio law she was as guilty as the actual killer, was sentenced to death, and the Court upheld the sentence. But her accomplice, the killer, had plea-bargained, and received a prison sentence.

In a previous chapter we described the case of Charles Brooks, Jr., who was executed by lethal injection (although his appeal was pending) while his partner, pleading guilty, got forty years with possible parole in six. Then, six weeks later, on January 25, 1983, the same Supreme Court issued a stay of execution to a Thomas A. Barefoot under almost identical circumstances of pending appeal.

All of the above seems to prove that our highest court has been and is in a state of confusion because of a lack of consensus among the justices about the issue of capital punishment. The only body that seems to have resolved the question (according to polls) is the majority of the American public. Unfortunately, it is equipped with a minimum of facts and a maximum of mass media indoctrination. Consequently, the majority opt for the finality of capital punishment. In contrast, we hope that our summation and what you've already read will help you arrive at a decision based upon a far broader viewpoint.

8

NOW, WHAT'S YOUR CONCLUSION?

We've come a long way in our comparatively brief study of the pros and cons of capital punishment. From ancient times, our British heritage, our colonial period, to today. You were introduced to the various and often conflicting theories about the causes of criminal behavior. To some degree it can be caused by nature (inherited traits), but in large part it is the result of nurture, the social-environmental pressures. You've been made aware of the rather disillusioning fact that our criminal court system's ways of dispensing justice are often the result of tipped scales. You've learned that our Supreme Court has been and probably will continue to be somewhat less than supreme in wisdom. The justices are essentially political appointees who bring with them not only their judicial experience but also, in some instances, their own prejudices, and their own vulnerability to public pressure. You have also been exposed to a number of statistics that appear to deny the deterrent effect of the death penalty. But, unlike the Canadian and British governments (both of which abandoned capital punishment), who allocated the necessary funds for statistical research, our government has not done so. Consequently our factual data is limited.

Everything you've read about the subject has been in abstract form (theories, opinions, statistics). Before you decide that you're for or against the death penalty, it might be helpful to vicariously experience what actually transpires at an execution. Here are the shocking details of what happened on December 12, 1984. A black criminal, Alpha Otis Stephens, was executed in Georgia. However, the first charge of electricity failed to do its job properly and the condemned man struggled to breathe for eight minutes before another charge was administered. How much did he suffer? Here's an excerpt from an eyewitness account of an electrocution by Don Reid, a Texas news reporter.

"The man is pale, His arms are lashed to arm rests, his legs to the chair legs, his body to the chair with a broad strap so taut that it straightens his spine to the chair back.

"He smiles—but he tries to cringe away as a guard stuffs cotton in his nostrils to trap blood that might gush from ruptured veins in his brain.

"A mask is placed across his face. The guard steps back quickly. The warden turns and nods in the direction of the one-way mirror behind which [the executioner] is waiting.

"The crunch. The mounting whine and snarl of the generator. The man's lips peel back, the throat strains for a last desperate cry, the body arches against the restraining straps . . . the features purple, steam and smoke rise from bald spots on head and leg while the sick-sweet smell of burned flesh permeates the little room."

Conclusion?

BIBLIOGRAPHY

Bedau, Hugo A., ed. *The Death Penalty in America.* 3d ed. New York: Oxford University Press, 1982.

Berger, Raoul. *Death Penalties.* Cambridge Mass.: Harvard University Press, 1982.

Black, Charles L., Jr. *Capital Punishment* rev. ed. New York: W. W. Norton & Co., 1982.

Bowers, William J., and Glenn L. Pierce. *Legal Homicide.* Boston: Northeastern University Press, 1983.

Calvert, Roy E. *Capital Punishment in the Twentieth Century.* 5th rev. ed. Montclair, N.J.: Patterson Smith Publishing Co., 1973.

Clear, Todd R., and George F. Cole. *American Corrections.* Monterey, Calif.: Brooks/Cole Publishing Co., 1986.

Cole, George F. *The American System of Criminal Justice.* 4th ed. Monterey, Calif.: Brooks/Cole Publishing Co., 1986.

Conrad, John P., and Ernest van den Haag. *The Death*

Penalty: A Debate. New York: Plenum Publishing Co., 1983.

Jackson, Robert H. *The Struggle for Judicial Supremacy.* New York: Octagon Books, 1979.

Schur, Edwin M. *Our Criminal Society.* Englewood Cliffs, N.J.: Prentice-Hall, 1969.

Schwed, Roger E. *Abolition and Capital Punishment.* New York: AMS Press, 1983.

Shin, Kilman. *Death Penalty and Crime.* Cullowhee, N.C.: Center for Economic Analysis, 1978.

Wilson, James Q., and Richard J. Hernstein. *Crime and Human Nature.* New York: Simon & Schuster, 1985.

INDEX

Spenkelink, John, 10
Stephens, Alpha Otis, 13, 86
Stoning, *19*
Supreme Court
    capital punishment rulings,
      14–15, 77, 79–80, 83–84
    confusion about capital
      punishment, 83–84
    constitutional interpretation
      by, 14–15, 79–80
    fallibility of, 76
    justices of, 75
    property rights rulings, 75–76

Torture, *20*, 21

Van den Haag, Ernest, 40, 63–65

Wars, 32
White, Dan, 80, 83
William the Conqueror, 22
Wilson, James Q., 40–41
Wilson, Margaret, 24
Witches, execution of, 23, *25*
Wolfgang, Marvin E., 72
Women, execution of 23–24, *25*
Woodson v. *North Carolina*, 83

ABOUT THE AUTHORS

Robert H. Loeb, Jr., was born in New York City but spent his childhood years in Switzerland. He attended Brown University and Columbia University. His book *New England Village* was selected as one of the outstanding social studies books for children in 1976. He has written a number of books for young people about how to cope with, instead of accepting, social and attitudinal problems. Now living and writing in his Connecticut home, he remains deeply interested in sociological problems, chiefly those of young people. His other Franklin Watts books are *Your Legal Rights as a Minor, Your Guide to Voting, Breaking the Sex-Role Barrier,* and *Marriage for Better or for Worse?*

George F. Cole is Professor of Political Science at The University of Connecticut. He is the author of: *Politics and the Administration of Justice, Criminal Justice: Law and Politics, The American System of Criminal Justice* and many other studies of the criminal justice system.